Fragrant as a Flower

I Wonder Why

Fragrant
as a
Flower

By Lawrence F. Lowery

Illustrated by June Goldsborough

NSTA Kids
National Science Teachers Association
Arlington, Virginia

Claire Reinburg, Director
Wendy Rubin, Managing Editor
Rachel Ledbetter, Associate Editor
Amanda Van Beuren, Associate Editor
Donna Yudkin, Book Acquisitions Coordinator

ART AND DESIGN
Will Thomas Jr., Director
Joseph Butera, Cover, Interior Design
Original illustrations by June Goldsborough

PRINTING AND PRODUCTION
Catherine Lorrain, Director

NATIONAL SCIENCE TEACHERS ASSOCIATION
David L. Evans, Executive Director
David Beacom, Publisher

1840 Wilson Blvd., Arlington, VA 22201
www.nsta.org/store
For customer service inquiries, please call 800-277-5300.

Lexile® measure: 610L

Library of Congress Cataloging-in-Publication Data

Names: Lowery, Lawrence F., author. | National Science Teachers Association, publisher. | Lowery, Lawrence F. I wonder why reader.
Title: Fragrant as a flower : I wonder why / by Larry Lowery.
Description: Arlington, VA : NSTA Kids, [2016] | Series: I wonder why | Audience: K to grade 3.
Identifiers: LCCN 2016036304 (print) | LCCN 2016036924 (ebook) | ISBN 9781681403533 (print) | ISBN 9781681403588 (e-book)
Subjects: LCSH: Smell--Juvenile literature. | Odors--Juvenile literature. | Senses and sensation--Juvenile literature.
Classification: LCC QP458 .L67 2016 (print) | LCC QP458 (ebook) | DDC 612.8/6--dc23
LC record available at https://lccn.loc.gov/2016036304

Introduction

The *I Wonder Why* series is a set of science books created specifically for young learners who are in their first years of school. The content for each book was chosen to be appropriate for youngsters who are beginning to construct knowledge of the world around them. These youngsters ask questions. They want to know about things. They are more curious than they will be when they are a decade older. Research shows that science is students' favorite subject when they enter school for the first time.

Science is both *what* we know and *how* we come to know it. What we know is the content knowledge that accumulates over time as scientists continue to explore the universe in which we live. How we come to know science is the set of thinking and reasoning processes we use to get answers to the questions and inquiries in which we are engaged.

Scientists learn by observing, comparing, and organizing the objects and ideas they are investigating. Children learn the same way. The thinking processes are among several inquiry behaviors that enable us to find out about our world and how it works. Our five senses—sight, hearing, touch, smell, and taste—provide our brains with information about our world. The senses enable us to distinguish one object or event from another. They help us successfully navigate our world, interpret our environment, and understand what's happening around us. They warn us of dangers and provide us with pleasant memories.

Each of our senses has its own neural operating system. Each sense organ—the eye, the ear, the skin, the nose, and the tongue—takes in environmental information through specialized cells with sensory receptors. That information is transformed into electrical signals that can be read by the brain. These signals are processed in their own respective areas of the brain, which then integrates this sensory information and puts the pieces together. The brain uses the information your senses provide to form useful representations that tell you how to best interact with your environment.

These books about our senses do not try to explain how senses work, but rather present information to sharpen the reader's awareness of his or her senses and help develop the skills that aid in gathering information and extending perceptions. *Fragrant as a Flower* explores smells. We smell with our noses, and smells can conjure memories of events and often involve emotions. *Quiet as a Butterfly* emphasizes that we hear and learn with our ears. *Look and See* introduces the richness of sight. Seeing with our eyes is a powerful sense for learning about the world around us. How and how well we know about something depend on the skill and thoroughness with which we use our senses.

Books in this series use different approaches to take the reader through simple, real-world information. One book is expository, providing factual information. A couple are narratives that take the reader on journeys of the senses. Different literary ways of presenting information bring the content to the reader through a variety of instructional avenues. The illustrations add detail and sometimes humor.

Unlike didactic presentations of knowledge, the content is woven into each book through the reader's point of view. The content is subtle but powerful and memorable, not memorizable. The science activities in the Parent/Teacher Handbook at the back of each book enable learners to conduct their own investigations related to the content. The materials needed for these activities are easily obtained, and the activities have been tested with youngsters to be sure they are age appropriate. After the reader completes a science activity, rereading or referring to the book and talking about connections with the activity can be a deepening experience that stabilizes the learning as a long-term memory.

My dad likes to tell stories.
One story he tells is about his walk around town
when he was my age. He had fun exploring smells.

Dad said, "On my walk around town
I saw a pastry shop.
What a good smell.
It made me stop.

Cookies and pies,
and sweet-smelling cakes,
and blueberry muffins
the baker makes."

Dad liked the smells of the pastry store,
so he sniffed and smelled and walked some more.

"What an odd smell," he said
as he came to a stop.
"Do you know what I smelled?" he asked.
"The local pet shop."

"Inside there were birds and fish,
and kittens and cats,
and three brown puppies
at play on the mats.

The smell of the animals is a pleasant smell.
I remember that pet shop very well."

Then Dad smelled a smell
as he passed by a door
"Do you know what it was?
It was a large tire store."

"There were tires," Dad said,
"for big cars and small.
And more tires," he said with a laugh,
"for trucks that are tall!"

My dad continued his story.

"What was that next smell?" he wondered.
"I'll have to think very hard."

"I know!" he said a bit later.
"Across the street is a lumberyard.
Pinewood and oak,
and maple, too.
There was walnut and cedar
and the smell of wood glue."

I've been to a lumberyard with my dad
and smelled the smells he remembers.
Perhaps someday I'll tell my kid
about the smells I remember.

I asked my dad if there was any smell he did not like.
He said, "Yes. I smelled a bad smell
and wrinkled my nose.
It was an old wooden cart
filled with wrinkled old clothes.

Scraps, rags,
and dirty bags.
Rubbish in a clump,
all smelled ready
for the dump."

I learned the smells that I don't like
are the same smells my dad dislikes.

Dad said, "Another smell I didn't like
was as bad as any I found.
Men were digging
a big hole in the ground."

"Dust and dirt
blew in my face.
Men with shovels
dug all over the place."

Dad next smelled something
that was pleasant but not sweet.
He said in his day they poured tar
on the street.

The tar was thick
and black and hot.
It's the best material to cover
a street's bad spots.

I don't know what tar smells like,
but I'd like to know.
My dad's stories make me wish
I lived long ago.

Another smell I'd like to learn
was part of Dad's story
when he came near a turn.

He said, "In a shoemaker's shop,
something smelled good.
I went inside and smelled the smells
where I stood."

Dad smelled old shoes,
new leather, and rubber heels.
He smelled brown polish and oil
on the shoemaker's wheel.

Dad said, "The air all around
smelled a bit like the shore."
A fish shop stood near,
and he peeked through the door.

There were codfish and sunfish
and fresh lobster tails.
He saw bluefish, butterfish,
and glass jars of snails.

As Dad walked,

a sweet country smell was on every side.

It came from a fruit shop

with doors open wide.

Dad smelled apples and oranges,

bananas and berries,

peaches and melons,

plums, pears, and cherries.

In my dad's story the next smell
was as sweet as fairyland.
It came through the air
from a lovely flower stand.

He smelled violets and daisies,
lilies and roses,
sunflowers, tulips,
and all kinds of posies.

Dad said, "There was a smell
as I neared my home.
It was the smell of clean laundry
swish-swashing in foam.

The smell of bleach,
soap suds, and cloth,
tumbling around
in bright, bubbly froth."

On the first day of spring
I walked through the park.
The smell of rain was still in the air.
Everywhere that I pass
I smell the fresh grass.
A smell in the air can tell me what's there.

A popcorn wagon
is around the corner.
I knew it
before I could see it.

Everywhere I go
there is a new smell to know.

I've learned a lot
from stories told by my dad.
Now I pay attention to smells
and that makes me glad.

Parent/Teacher Handbook

Introduction

In *Fragrant as a Flower*, a father tells his son about exploring smells in town when he was his son's age. His son associates his own experiences with the smells his dad remembers and realizes that smells often help us recall experiences. The son also notes that some smells are connected to certain times in the past and can no longer be experienced in the same way. The walk his dad describes involves memories of visits to a fish market, pastry shop, lumberyard, fruit stand, and shoemaker, as well as of various activities along the street.

Inquiry Processes

Like some other books in this series, this book emphasizes an individual aspect of observation. *Fragrant as a Flower* describes how the sense of smell provides important information about our environment. The father describes how he used his sense of smell to make observations about things present around him before he saw them.

Although smells are emphasized in this book, observations are always multisensory. We use all of our senses to report experiences accurately.

Content

We take in information about events through our senses. Although each sense follows its own pathway into our brain, our brain integrates the information to give us a holistic sense of an event. For our sense of smell, odors are tiny, invisible particles (molecules) in gaseous form that travel through the air to the sense organs of smell located between our eyes in our nasal cavity. Hairlike cells in our nose serve as smell detectors. When stimulated by odor molecules, these cells send signals to various brain regions, which produce the sensation of odors.

Odors are difficult to classify into definite types. Each substance has a distinct smell, and descriptions of smells are usually descriptions of the objects that produce the smell (e.g., "It smells like chocolate," or "It has a lemon smell.").

There are many different kinds of receptors. Each is specific for a particular kind of odor. The range of human sensitivity to odors is wide for some people and narrow for others. Some people lack a sense of smell for certain odors. Others have a highly sensitive sense of smell. Smell also has a strong capacity to bring back memories.

Science Activities

Note: Before doing these activities, be sure to check with the school nurse about any potential allergy or asthma issues.

Identifying Smells

Many items can be used to help readers experience different smells. Several items are suggested, but be careful if you try others. Some people are allergic to some smells (e.g., scented soaps), and some substances that smell are hazardous and shouldn't be used (e.g., rubbing alcohol). The following activities provide several ways to experience different smells.

1. Go on a "smelling walk" and write or draw pictures of the experiences in a story form. Any neighborhood has wonderful sources of smells for the purpose of describing

and identifying different smells. (Make sure the field trip location does not have any potential safety issues.)

2. Clean ketchup and mustard squeeze bottles are useful for identifying some smells. Put cotton balls prepared with different smells in different bottles. Use your imagination—perhaps dampen the cotton balls with extracts such as lemon, mint, or vanilla. Or add some cinnamon, nutmeg, or garlic to the bottles. You could also put slices of orange, lemon, or banana in the bottles. Remember that when working with food, you should be aware of any foods that may cause allergic reactions, and remind students not to eat any of the food used.

Once you've put a smell in the bottle, you can squeeze the bottle to experience the smell. (Remind students to keep the pointed nozzle away from their eyes.) If you place the sources of the smell (or pictures of the sources) on a table, you can ask the reader to place the bottle next to the picture or object that it smells like. Let the reader describe how she could do this. Have the reader find pictures in this book where the different smells might be found.

3. Various liquids can be identified by the reader with closed eyes. Caution the reader against inhaling deeply or placing his nostrils directly over strong-smelling substances. Again, use your imagination. Some substances that can be used are banana oil, vanilla extract, lemon extract, orange extract, and soy sauce. After each substance has been identified, ask the reader some questions:

- What does the smell make you think of?
- Is the substance used in cooking, in cleaning, to make things smell nice, or for another reason?
- Does the smell come from something that grows or something that is made?

Locating the Source of a Smell

Hide an aromatic substance such as an open perfume bottle in a room. Have the reader use her sense of smell to track it down.

Matching Solid Objects by the Sense of Smell

Our ability to detect different smells and match identical smells can be improved by experiencing activities that involve the matching of objects by their aromas.

Provide the reader with six to eight bars of soap that have different scents, and place these bars in containers such as empty jars or bowls. (Scented candles can be used as an alternative to bars of soap.) The bars should be identical in size and shape and wrapped so that they cannot be distinguished on the basis of color. Place one more bar matching one of the scents in another container and ask the reader to find the matching container within the set using his sense of smell. As a variation of this activity, you can mix the boxes and ask the reader to find the two that smell alike.

For a more challenging variation of this activity, prepare two of these sets of containers with soap, mix them up, and ask the reader to pair up all of the containers according to smell.

Matching Liquids by the Sense of Smell

This activity demonstrates how our sense of smell can distinguish between liquids better than our sense of sight. Prepare two baby food jars. Jar #1 should have water and Jar #2 should have white vinegar. (The amounts should be the same.) Have the reader note that these liquids look the same. Have her smell the bottles. What does she notice? (They smell different even though they look the same.)

Now have her sniff another prepared set, using jars of red vinegar, white vinegar, and cider vinegar (or just use white vinegar in each, but color each with different food colorings). Have her note that these all look different. Ask what she noticed after smelling them. (They all smell the same but look different.)